D1441133

FOR HEARTS THAT HURT

Zondervan Gifts

For Hearts That Hurt
Copyright 1997 by The Zondervan Corporation
ISBN 0-310-97058-X

Printed In China

Requests for information should be addressed to:

 ZondervanPublishingHouse

Grand Rapids, Michigan 49530
http://www.zondervan.com

Senior Editor: Joy Marple
Project Editor: Sarah Hupp
Art Director: Robin Welsh
Designer: Christopher Tobias/Tobias Design
Photographer: Dennis Frates/Oregon Scenics

Some quotations for this book were taken from the following:
Eleanor Doan, THE COMPLETE SPEAKERS SOURCEBOOK, Zondervan Publishing House, 1996; p. 3,8,41,46.
Robert I. Fitzhenry, ed., THE HARPER BOOK OF QUOTATIONS, 3rd ed., HarperPerennial, a division of HarperCollins Publishers, 1993; p. 33,34,47.
Frank S. Mead, ed., 12,000 RELIGIOUS QUOTATIONS, Baker Book House, 1989; p. 5,7,10, 13,16,17,20,22,24,26,31,38,40,42,43,45,47,48.
James Dalton Morrison, ed., MASTERPIECES OF RELIGIOUS VERSE, Baker Book House, 1977; p. 12,24,27,44,48.
Robert Schuller, POWER THOUGHTS, HarperCollins Publishers, 1993; p. 19,21,25,35,38.
George Sweeting, WHO SAID THAT?, Moody Press, 1995; p. 1,2,9,14,37.
R.E.O. White, YOU CAN SAY THAT AGAIN, Zondervan Publishing House, 1991; p. 2,5,6, 7,13,14,18,20,22,29,31,33,39,40,42,47.

To: Sharlee and Don,

No one knows the true weight of another's burden,
but God gave us the shoulders of friends to lean on.

From: Marsha Marshall

April 1, 1997

Surely God is my salvation;
I will trust and not be afraid.

—Isaiah 12:2a

BUT GOD

I know not, but God knows;
Oh, blessed rest from fear!
All my unfolding days
To him are plain and clear.

I cannot, but God can;
Oh, balm for all my care!
The burden that I drop
His hand will lift and bear,
Though eagle pinions tire
I walk where once I ran,

THIS IS MY STRENGTH TO KNOW:
I CANNOT, BUT GOD CAN.

—ANNIE JOHNSON FLINT

It is far, far more God who must hold us, than we who must hold him.

—FRIEDRICH VON HUGEL

The feeble hands and helpless
          Groping out into the darkness
Touch God's right hand in that darkness,
          And are lifted up and strengthened.

—HENRY WADSWORTH LONGFELLOW

Blessed are those who mourn, for they will be comforted.

—MATTHEW 5:4

God does not take away the darkness, but he guides us through it.

Gray skies . . .
     a hurting heart . . .
          somber words.
Dark despair, thickened like storm clouds.
     Yet
How would one recognize dark . . .
     If there were no light to compare?
     So . . .
Illumine, Lord!

—SARAH MICHAELS

Adversity is the diamond dust
with which Heaven polishes its jewels.

—ROBERT LEIGHTON

HE LEADS US ON

He leads us on
By paths we do not know;
Upwards he leads us, though our steps be slow;
Though oft we faint and falter on the way,
Though storms and darkness oft obscure the day,
Yet, when the clouds are gone,
We know He leads us on.

—HIRAM O. WILEY

There is wondrous healing in rest and patience, and a depth of meaning we have never yet fathomed in the words of the prophet, "In quietness and trust is your strength." (Isaiah 30:15)

Whenever God gives us a cross to bear, it is a prophecy that he will also give us strength.

P E A C E that the world has not to give

Is theirs who do the Savior's will;

Help Thou us more to Him to live,

And with His peace our spirits fill.

—JOHN E. BODE

WHAT, THEN, SHALL WE SAY . . . ?

**IF GOD IS FOR US,
WHO CAN BE AGAINST US?**

—ROMANS 8:31

*Wherever one walks faithfully
in the way that God has marked out for him,
God will be on that one's side.*
—after Henry Ward Beecher

Therefore we do not lose heart. Though outwardly we are wasting away, yet inwardly we are being renewed day by day. For our light and momentary troubles are achieving for us an eternal glory that far outweighs them all.

—2 Corinthians 4:16-17

He Has A Plan

As I walk along life's pathway,

Though the way I cannot see

I shall follow in his footsteps,
For he has a plan for me.

So I look to him for guidance,

Savior, Lord and King is he;

I can trust him aye, forever,
Since he has a plan for me!

—ROSELLA THIESEN

LORD, GIVE ME FAITH!

Lord, give me faith to trust, if not to know;
With quiet mind in all things thee to find,
And, child-like, to go where thou wouldst have
me go.

—JOHN OXENHAM

*Trust God where you cannot trace him. Do not
try to penetrate the cloud he brings over you;
rather look to the rainbow that is on it.
The mystery is God's; the promise is yours.*

—JOHN MACDUFF

May our Lord Jesus Christ . . . who loved us an
by his grace gave us eternal encouragement and
good hope, encourage your hearts and strength
you in every good deed and word.

—2 THESSALONIANS 2:16-17

Behind the cloud the starlight lurks,
 Through showers the sunbeams fall;
For God, who loveth all his works,
 Has left his hope for all.

—JOHN GREENLEAF WHITTIER

Other men see only a hopeless end, but
the Christian rejoices in an endless hope.

—GILBERT M. BEENKEN

In your unfailing love you will lead
the people you have redeemed.

—Exodus 15:13

Although today he prunes my twigs with pain,
        Yet doth His blood nourish and warm my root:
Tomorrow I shall put forth buds again,
        And clothe myself with fruit.
—Christina Rossetti

It's not what happens to us, but what happens in us that supremely counts.

And the God of all grace, who called you to his eternal glory in
Christ, after you have suffered a little while, will himself restore you
and make you strong, firm and steadfast.
—1 Peter 5:10

O God, *help us to trust in thee at all times,*

and never to doubt thy promises and love.

In our duties, **grant us thy help;**

in our dangers, **thy protection;**

in our difficulties, **thy guidance;**

AND IN OUR SORROW, THY PEACE.

May thy grace be sufficient for us,

and thy strength made perfect in our weakness;

and bring us at last to thine eternal kingdom,

through Jesus Christ our Lord. Amen.

—UNKNOWN

Be strong and take heart,
all you who hope in the Lord.

—Psalm 31:24

*Wait for the LORD; be strong and take heart
and wait for the LORD*

—PSALM 27:14

TRUST

Build a little fence of trust

Around today;

Fill the space with loving work,

And therein stay;

Look not through the sheltering bars

Upon tomorrow;

God will help thee bear what comes

Of joy or sorrow.

—Mary Frances Butts

God tempers the wind to the shorn lamb.

—Laurence Sterne

Let shadows come, let shadows go
Let life be bright or full of woe
I am content for this I know:
Thou thinkest, Lord, of me.

*For a little while you may have had to
suffer grief in all kinds of trials. These have
come so that your faith—of greater worth
than gold, which perishes even though
refined by fire—may be proved genuine and
may result in praise, glory and honor when
Jesus Christ is revealed.*

—1 PETER 1:6-7

The LORD is my light and my salvation-
whom shall I fear? The LORD is the
stronghold of my life of whom shall I
be afraid?

—PSALM 27:1

Trust God for great things; with your
five loaves and two fishes, he will show
you a way to feed thousands.

—HORACE BUSHNELL

"For I know the plans I have for you," declares the Lord, "plans to prosper you and not to harm you, plans to give you hope and a future."

—JEREMIAH 29:11

Hope is the power of being cheerful in circumstances which we know to be desperate.

—G. K. Chesterton

Storms always lose to the sun. The sunrise always overtakes the night . . . and winter always turns into spring. Impossible situations can become possible miracles.

—Robert Schuller

I can do everything through him who gives me strength.
—Philippians 4:13

Nobody knows the trouble I've seen,

Nobody knows my sorrow.

Nobody knows the trouble I've seen,

NOBODY KNOWS BUT JESUS.

—Negro Spiritual

Why are you downcast, O my soul?
Why so disturbed within me?
Put your hope in God,
for I will yet praise him, my Savior and my God.
—Psalm 42:11

He knows the way I take;
when he has tested me, I will come forth as gold.
My feet have closely follwed his steps;
I have kept to his way without turning aside.

—JOB 23:10–13

The future is as bright as the promises of God.

—WILLIAM CAREY

Drop thy still dews of quietness,

Till all our strivings cease;

Take from our souls the strain and stress,

AND LET OUR ORDERED LIVES CONFESS,

THE BEAUTY OF THY PEACE.

—JOHN GREENLEAF WHITTIER

The LORD gives strength to his people;
the LORD blesses his people with peace.

—PSALM 29:11

Never make an irreversible decision in a down time. Are you ill? Are you filled with grief? Have you just had a terrible argument with your spouse? . . . Don't let your emotions make your decisions. Don't let your temper rule your life. Tough times pass. Tough people survive. Rest. Wait. Now is not the time to make an irreversible decision. Reserve your judgment until the sun is shining.

—ROBERT SCHULLER

Cast your cares on the LORD and he will sustain you; he will never let the righteous fall.

—PSALM 55:22

I am convinced that neither death nor life,
neither angels nor demons, neither the
present nor the future, nor any powers,
neither height nor depth, nor anything
else in all creation, will be able to separate
us from the love of God that is in Christ
Jesus our Lord.

—ROMANS 8:38-39

We can better appreciate the miracle
of a sunrise if we have waited in darkness.

The LORD your God is with you, he is mighty to save.
He will take great delight in you, he will quiet you
with his love, he will rejoice over you with singing.
—Zephaniah 3:17

IT IS THE LORD

Sometimes a light surprises
The Christian while he sings;
It is the Lord who rises
With healing in his wings;
When comforts are declining
He grants the soul again
A season of clear shining
To cheer it after rain.

—WILLIAM COWPER

*Life has burdens that no one can escape. Christ does not remove
the load: he teaches us how best to bear the burdens that fall
rightfully to us.*

"With everlasting kindness I will have compassion on you,
says the Lord your Redeemer."

—ISAIAH 54:8B

THE HOPE OF MY LIFE

Just when the night is the darkest,

When hope is the farthest from sight,

God's light floods the depths of my
pain-wracked soul
And turns my despair to life.

His grace brings the deepest of comforts;

His presence envelops my pain.

THE HOPE OF MY LIFE REVEALS HIS DEAR FACE

AND BRINGS ME TO WHOLENESS AGAIN.

—MICHAEL SARAI

Weeping may remain for a night,
but rejoicing comes in the morning.
—Psalm 30:5b

*You will keep in perfect peace him whose mind is steadfast,
because he trusts in you.*

—Isaiah 26:3

Strong in the Lord of Hosts,
And in his mighty power;

Who in the strength of Jesus trusts

Is more than conqueror.

STAND, THEN, IN HIS GREAT MIGHT,

WITH ALL HIS STRENGTH ENDUED;

And take, to arm you for the fight,

The covering of God.

—CHARLES WESLEY

Trust in the LORD with all your heart and lean not on your own understanding; in all your ways acknowledge him, and he will make your paths straight.

—PROVERBS 3:5-6

Guide me, O thou great Redeemer
Pilgrim through this barren land;
I am weak, but thou are mighty,
Hold me with thy powerful hand;
Bread of heaven,
Feed me till I want no more.

—WILLIAM WILLIAMS

The joy of the LORD is your strength.

—NEHEMIAH 8:10B

Often the clouds of sorrow reveal the
sunshine of God's face.

—HILYS JASPER

The LORD bless you and keep you; the
LORD make his face shine upon you and
be gracious to you; the LORD turn his
face toward you and give you peace.

—NUMBERS 6:24-26

If the sun of God's countenance shine upon me,
I may well be content to be wet
with the rain of affliction.

—JOSEPH HALL

So, darkness in the pathway of man's life
Is but the shadow of God's providence,
By the great Sun of Wisdom cast thereon;
And what is dark below is light in heaven.

—JOHN GREENLEAF WHITTIER

The Lord gives strength to his people; the Lord blesses his people with peace,

—PSALM 29:11

Extraordinary afflictions are not always the punishment of extraordinary sins, but sometimes the trial of extraordinary graces.

—MATTHEW HENRY

So we fix our eyes not on what is seen, but on what is unseen.

For what is seen is temporary, but what is unseen is eternal.

—2 Corinthians 4:18

Think not thou canst sigh a sigh

And thy Maker is not by;

Think not thou canst weep a tear

And thy Maker is not near.

O! He gives to us His joy

That our grief He may destroy.

—William Blake